7 paint pots

8 apples

9 boats

10 socks

How you can help

First Steps *123* helps children to recognise the numbers 1–10 by linking numbers with colourful photographs of familiar objects. Important concepts such as matching, sorting and ordering are introduced in an entertaining way.

 Help your child to say the number and trace over the number shapes with her finger.

 Enjoy talking about the photographs together. What is the same? What is different? Are the boots the same colour as her* own boots?, etc.

There are lots of other ways to help your child learn about numbers. Use rhymes and games to practise saying numbers out loud. Make number shapes from play dough or pastry.

Colouring, tidying up and shopping all provide excellent opportunities for counting and sorting.

*To avoid the clumsy 'he/she',
the child is referred to throughout as 'she'.

Ladybird would like to thank Priscilla Hannaford, freelance editor on this series.

A catalogue record for this book is available
from the British Library

Published by Ladybird Books Ltd
A subsidiary of the Penguin Group
A Pearson Company
© LADYBIRD BOOKS LTD MCMXCVII

LADYBIRD and the device of a Ladybird are trademarks of
Ladybird Books Ltd Loughborough Leicestershire UK

123

by Lesley Clark
photography by Garie Hind

Ladybird

 one

one teddy bear

2 two

two boots

3 three

three cars

4 four

four ducks

5 five

five toothbrushes

6 six

six building blocks

7 seven

seven paint pots

8 eight

eight apples

 nine

nine boats

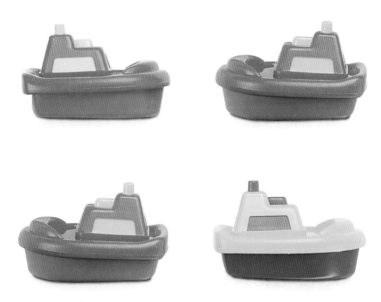

Encourage your child to point to each boat as she counts it.

10 ten

ten socks

Count the socks and try to match the pairs on the line. You could do this at home with real socks or other objects.

What can you see in this bag?

How many of each thing?

Can you help to unpack
the shopping?

Is everything here?

Here's the washing to sort out.

Let's get everything out of the basket.

How many T-shirts can you count?

How many socks?

Each of these boxes has three ducks in it. Can you count them?

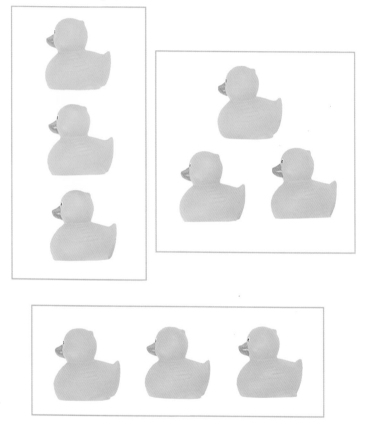

Play games with buttons and other objects to help your child to understand that the number stays the same no matter how the objects are arranged.

How many drinks are there?

Is there a straw for each drink?

How many horses are on the farm?

How many cows?

How many geese?

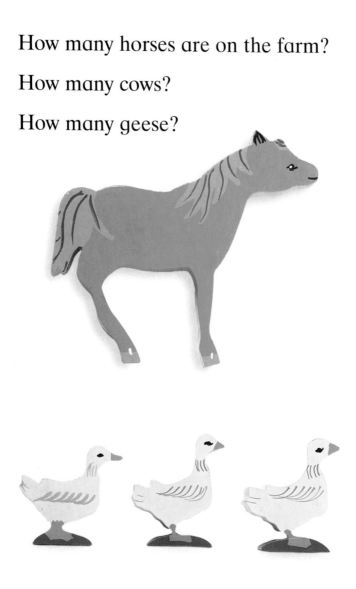

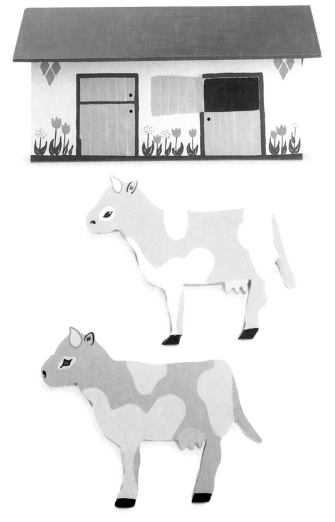

Count up all the animals and say
how many there are altogether.

These four cars drive round
and round.

These four are home –
safe and sound.

What games do you play with
your cars?

How many balls?

Which is the largest?

Which is the smallest?

Talk about the different sizes and colours of the balls.

Can you count how many flowers?

Which one is different from all
the others?

Yum! How many green diamonds are on the cake?

How many red diamonds?

How many diamonds are there altogether?

First Steps

Aimed at children aged 2 years and upwards, the **First Steps** range of mini hardback books, activity books and flash cards are designed to complement one another and can be used in any order.

mini hardbacks

- abc
- 123
- colours and shapes
- sorting and opposites
- time

  Durable hardback books use photographs and illustrations to introduce important early learning concepts.

from **First Steps** *abc*